A **TRUE** BOOK

P9-CFJ-151

Energy

MATT MULLINS

Children's Press®
An Imprint of Scholastic Inc.
New York Toronto London Auckland Sydney
Mexico City New Delhi Hong Kong
Danbury, Connecticut

Content Consultant
Suzanne E. Willis, PhD
Professor and Assistant Chair, Department of Physics
Northern Illinois University
DeKalb, Illinois

Library of Congress Cataloging-in-Publication Data

Mullins, Matt.
  Energy/Matt Mullins.
    p. cm.—(A true book)
  Includes bibliographical references and indexes.
  ISBN-13: 978-0-531-26320-4 (lib. bdg.)   ISBN-10: 0-531-26320-7 (lib. bdg.)
  ISBN-13: 978-0-531-26582-6 (pbk.)   ISBN-10: 0-531-26582-X (pbk.)
  1. Force and energy—Juvenile literature. I. Title.
  QC73.4.M85 2012
  531'.6—dc23   2011016234

All rights reserved. Published in 2012 by Children's Press, an imprint of Scholastic Inc.
Printed in China 62
SCHOLASTIC, CHILDREN'S PRESS, A TRUE BOOK, and associated logos are trademarks and/or registered trademarks of Scholastic Inc.
1 2 3 4 5 6 7 8 9 10 R 21 20 19 18 17 16 15 14 13 12

Find the Truth!

Everything you are about to read is true *except* for one of the sentences on this page.

Which one is **TRUE**?

T or F   The amount of energy in the world changes all the time.

T or F   Sound energy travels faster through water than through air.

Find the answers in this book.

Contents

1 Energy Is Everywhere

What does energy have to do with work? 7

2 Energy Is Ready!

What is potential energy? 13

3 Energy Travels

What is kinetic energy? 23

Kinetic energy

Swinging on a playground

THE **BIG** TRUTH!

Renewable Energy

How can we make sure we always have
enough energy? 26

4 Energy Changes and Stays the Same!

Can we create or destroy energy? 37

True Statistics 43

Resources 44

Important Words 46

Index 47

About the Author 48

Calories are a measurement of how much energy food contains.

5

You use energy
to play sports.

CHAPTER 1

Energy Is Everywhere

Energy is all around us. It's in your house as electricity. It's in your car as fuel. It's in sunlight. It's in the wind. It's everywhere!

Energy is the ability to do work. What is work? When you move a thing from one place to another, you do work. Picking up a heavy rock is work. So is moving the pedals on your bike or kicking a ball across the yard.

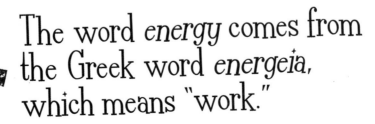

The word *energy* comes from the Greek word *energeia*, which means "work."

Even a tiny drop of water is made up of many molecules.

Atoms and Energy!

Energy is everywhere because it comes from atoms. Everything in the universe is made of atoms. When two or more atoms join together, they form a **molecule**. Water molecules, for example, contain two atoms of hydrogen and one atom of oxygen.

Inside atoms are tiny **protons**, **neutrons**, and **electrons**. Protons and neutrons stay inside the middle, or **nucleus**, of the atom. Electrons move around the nucleus.

Electrons have a negative electric charge. Protons have a positive electric charge. That is why electrons and protons are attracted to one another. This attraction is what holds atoms and molecules together. Sometimes electrons move away from an atom. When they do, they can become attracted to and join up with protons on another atom.

There is a lot of energy inside each tiny atom. Scientists believe that if they could release all the energy inside the atoms of 2 pounds (0.91 kilograms) of coal, they could power a whole country for weeks!

Electrons circle around the atom's nucleus.

The body of a 150-pound (68 kg) person contains a huge number of atoms— about 7 followed by 27 zeros!

Potential Energy

A lump of coal may not look like it is full of energy. You can't see the atoms moving in the coal. The energy they have is just sitting there. This is called **potential energy**. But we need something to act on the coal, such as fire, in order to use the energy. When coal burns, it releases energy.

Coal's energy makes it a powerful fuel source.

Coal is used to create about 41 percent of the world's electricity.

Kinetic Energy

Energy in motion is called **kinetic energy**. A ball that is sitting on the ground in your backyard has potential energy. It isn't moving. If you throw it, it has kinetic energy as it moves through the air. A rubber band has potential

This rubber band's potential energy will turn into kinetic energy once it is let go.

energy when you hold and stretch it. It has kinetic energy when it is moving through the air after you let it go.

The rock slide at Frank, Alberta in Canada turned the potential energy of gravity into kinetic energy.

CHAPTER 2

Energy Is Ready!

Potential energy comes in different forms. One kind of potential energy comes from gravity. A rock on a mountain has *gravitational energy*. When the rock rolls down the mountain, gravity pulls it. It bounces down the mountain, releasing energy every time it hits the ground. When the rock crashes at the bottom, it releases energy into the ground around it.

In 1903, the rock slide at Frank, Alberta, Canada, released 90 million tons of limestone in 100 seconds.

Gravitational Energy and You

You use gravitational energy when you play. You are releasing gravitational energy when you let go and slide down a slide at the playground. Sledding down a snowy hill uses gravitational energy in the same way. Bicycle down a hill, or ride on roller skates or a skateboard down a ramp, and the pull of gravity is at work.

Gravitational energy is what makes sledding fun.

Energy is measured in units called joules.

Like anything that moves, swings have energy.

Elastic Energy

When we stretch or squeeze things, we use another form of potential energy. It's called *elastic energy*. It is stored in things that stretch or squeeze, like rubber bands or springs. A rubber ball has a lot of elastic energy. So does a trampoline. A lot of the things you use on a playground hold elastic energy as well as gravitational energy. When you use a swing, for example, you pump your legs back and forth. This is using elastic energy. Gravitational energy pulls you back down to Earth.

Your food contains the energy your body needs to live.

Chemical Energy

Chemical energy is stored in many things. Chemical energy is energy stored in the bonds that hold molecules together. It is released when these bonds are broken apart. It is used by people and animals to live. All food holds chemical energy. When you eat broccoli, you release its chemical energy. A cow chews grass and releases the chemical energy in it. Your body contains chemicals that help release the energy of the food you eat.

Fuel also holds chemical energy. We use chemical energy in gas stoves, in cars, and in fireplaces.

Batteries are another source of chemical energy. A battery contains a mixture of chemicals that store energy. This mixture includes atoms that get excited easily. The electrons are ready to jump away when they are touched by metal. This releases chemical energy, powering the flashlight or other object to which the battery is attached.

Wood was the main source of energy in the United States until the 1800s. ➡

How Old Are Batteries?

We use batteries in many electronic devices, such as computers, game consoles, and remote controls for our televisions. We used to think the first battery was invented by Alessandro Volta in 1800. But in 1936, a clay pot was found near Baghdad, Iraq. It was almost 2,000 years old. It contained iron wrapped with copper. Scientists believe it was a battery. It was probably used to generate electricity!

Nuclear Energy

An atom's nucleus contains protons and neutrons. It also contains a tremendous amount of potential energy. The energy holds the protons and neutrons inside the nucleus. When released, this is called *nuclear energy*. The potential energy can be released in two ways. One way is to join a nucleus with another nucleus. When two or more nuclei (that's plural for nucleus!) combine, we call the process **fusion**.

Rutherford is known as the Father of Nuclear Physics.

Ernest Rutherford discovered the atomic nucleus in 1910.

Each star's light is caused by a release of energy.

Combining Atoms

Fusion is what keeps the sun burning. Inside the sun, hydrogen atoms combine with great force. This fusion releases a huge amount of energy. All the stars in the sky use fusion to create the light you see. The fusion of atoms is the most powerful way that we know of to release energy.

Splitting Atoms

The other way to release nuclear energy is to split a nucleus apart. Releasing nuclear energy this way is called **fission**. Nuclear power plants use fission to generate electricity. Fission splits atoms apart using a nuclear reaction. This creates large amounts of heat. Nuclear power plants use cooling systems to keep the reaction from burning out of control.

Nuclear power plants have large cooling towers to help release the heat created by nuclear fission.

The first nuclear power plant opened near Moscow, Russia, in 1954.

Vehicles being driven on highways generate lots of kinetic energy.

CHAPTER 3

Energy Travels

If objects at rest have potential energy, what about objects that are moving? When objects move, they have kinetic energy. When things move, they store energy. The faster something moves, the more energy it stores. A car traveling at 10 miles (16 kilometers) per hour has less kinetic energy than one going 30 miles per hour (48 kph). When an object slows down or stops, it releases the stored kinetic energy it has been building up.

 Cars turn the potential chemical energy of fuel into kinetic energy.

Blowing, Rolling, Crashing!

Think about wind. From inside a house, you may not know it is out there. What happens when you step outside? Wind stops against your body. You feel its kinetic energy. Roll a ball against a wall slowly, and it bounces off slowly. Roll it fast, and it bounces off fast. The energy is greater if the ball moves faster. If you have ever crashed on a bike, you know about kinetic energy!

Bowling balls use kinetic energy to knock over pins.

Large bells make louder noises than small bells, because they can vibrate more air than smaller ones can.

There is no sound in outer space. →

Sound Energy

Sound is another kind of energy. Sound travels through things like waves cross the ocean. When a force causes something to vibrate, sound energy is released. Strike a bell. Do you hear its energy waves traveling through the air? For sound to travel, it must have something to move through. Air is made up of molecules. Sound energy moves through the air molecules and causes them to vibrate.

Renewable Energy

We use different kinds of energy sources to generate the electricity we need. Some energy sources cannot be replaced. For example, there is only so much oil we can pump out of the ground. There is only so much coal we can dig up. Coal, oil, and natural gas are **nonrenewable** sources of energy. Other energy sources are **renewable**. Examples of these include wind, water, solar, and geothermal energy. Renewable sources of energy cannot be used up!

Geothermal energy is generated deep inside Earth's core.

The most common source of energy for producing electricity worldwide is nonrenewable coal.

Only about 8 percent of the energy used in the United States comes from renewable sources.

California's Mojave Desert has the world's biggest solar power plant.

The blue whale is both the largest and the loudest animal on Earth.

That's Loud!

Sound energy travels four times faster through water than through air. The loudest animal in the world lives in water—the blue whale. Its whistle is louder than a jet engine! The sound energy of the blue whale can travel through the ocean for hundreds of miles. Scientists are not sure how the whale makes this sound. They think blue whales move air quickly through cavities like the ones humans have behind their noses.

Radiant Energy

Like sound, light is a form of energy that travels in waves. It is one kind of *radiant energy*. The radiant energy of the sun brings warmth to Earth. It is used by plants to create food for themselves. Life on Earth is possible because of the radiant energy of the sun.

There are some kinds of radiant energy that cannot be seen by human eyes. We can't see radiant energy such as radio waves and X-rays.

Greenhouses help plants grow by trapping the heat from the sun during the day.

Thermal Energy

Heat is another kind of energy. It is known as *thermal energy*. Heat results when atoms and molecules vibrate and bump into one another. When you rub your hands together quickly, they get warm. The thermal energy you feel when rubbing your hands together comes from atoms on your skin bumping one another. The movement of the atoms in your hands generates heat.

Rubbing your hands together is a good way to keep warm when it is cold outside.

Volcanoes and hot springs are a result of natural heat energy from the center of the planet.

Lots of geothermal energy is stored in the area known as the Ring of Fire that surrounds the Pacific Ocean.

Thermal energy can come from inside Earth. Rock and metal are pushed together deep inside Earth's core. Rubbing and pushing makes these materials very hot. This geothermal energy heats water that comes out as steam from openings in Earth's crust. Some of the geothermal energy comes out when lava erupts from a volcano. Some of the energy heats natural hot springs.

Electrical Energy

When electrons flow through things such as wires, we call it electricity. This *electrical energy* can power devices we use every day. Lightbulbs, music players, televisions, and some kinds of cars and trains run on electricity.

Lightning is also a form of electrical energy. It happens when electrons build up in clouds. Sometimes electrons cause lightning in a cloud and light it up. Sometimes they cause a lightning bolt that flashes from the sky to the ground!

Energy Timeline

500–900
People in Persia use windmills to harness wind energy to pump water and grind grain.

1800
Alessandro Volta creates an early chemical battery.

Power Plants

People generate electricity at power plants. In power plants, a fuel such as coal heats water into steam. The steam from the water's thermal energy turns a turbine, or large fan. The turbine generates electricity as it turns. Wires carry this electricity to the people who need the power. Even nuclear power plants work this way. They use nuclear energy to heat water into steam.

1882
Thomas Edison opens the first power plant in New York City.

1968
A solar furnace using an eight-story mirror is built in France.

Electric eels are native to South America.

Electric eels use their electrical energy to stun their prey.

Electric Animals

Electric eels and certain kinds of fish have special cells in their bodies. These cells can generate electrical energy. Human bodies also generate electricity. Your brain sends tiny electrical signals to tell your muscles to move. The brain signals your heart to squeeze and release. The movement of the heart muscle pumps blood through your body.

Energy From Water

Water that moves fast has a lot of energy. Water that falls from a high point also has a lot of energy. The energy of moving water can be used to generate electricity. **Hydroelectric power** plants are places where the energy of water is converted to electricity. The Niagara River in New York supplies a lot of energy to people nearby. The power plant at Hoover Dam, in Nevada, is another well-known hydroelectric power plant.

Hoover Dam provides electricity to parts of California, Nevada, and Arizona.

Wax is the fuel that allows a candle to burn.

CHAPTER 4

Energy Changes and Stays the Same!

Energy changes form all the time. When you burn wood, it changes from chemical energy to thermal and radiant energy. The wood itself changes to ash as it burns. But no matter how many times energy changes form, the amount of energy never changes. You cannot create or destroy energy.

People in Greece used water power to grind grain more than 6,000 years ago.

Energy and You

Do you have energy? Of course! Here is an example. Imagine you are sitting at a table. There is an apple on the table. The apple contains chemical energy. You eat the apple. Your brain sends electricity to your jaw muscles. Your mouth chews. Chemicals in your stomach change the apple into chemical energy in your body. You go to a park and run. Your chemical energy is converted to heat and kinetic energy.

A huge amount of energy is transferred every time you do something as simple as eating an apple.

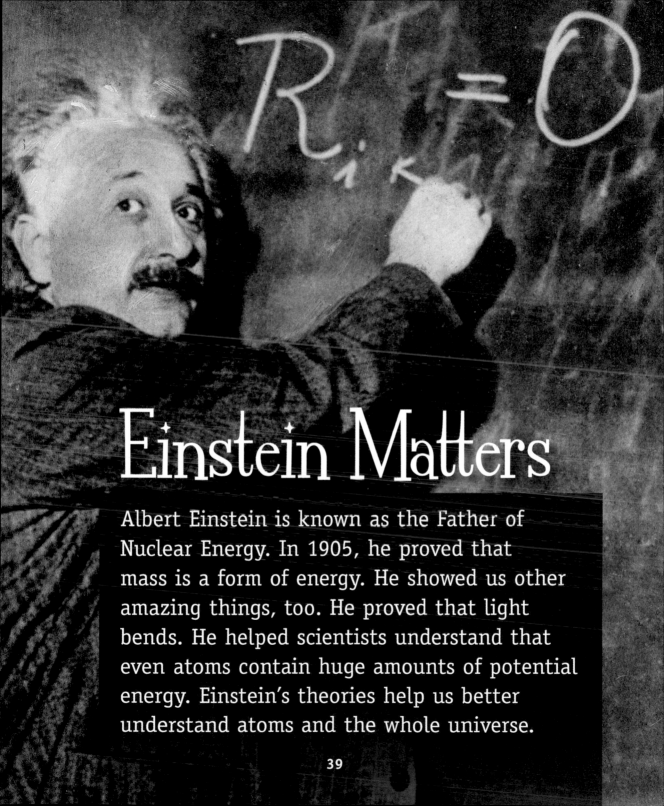

Einstein Matters

Albert Einstein is known as the Father of Nuclear Energy. In 1905, he proved that mass is a form of energy. He showed us other amazing things, too. He proved that light bends. He helped scientists understand that even atoms contain huge amounts of potential energy. Einstein's theories help us better understand atoms and the whole universe.

Think about how energy is being used next time you play at a park.

Conservation of Energy

Scientists call a contained group of things a system. A system can be as big as the universe or as small as an atom. Your body, the apple, and the park are a system. In this system, energy changes from chemical to electrical energy. It becomes kinetic energy in the park. But the amount of energy does not change.

Scientists call this the law of the conservation of energy. Energy in a system changes form, but the total amount of energy never changes. Scientists study ways to use energy efficiently. One way is to make the sun part of a system.

The United States consumes about 26 percent of the world's energy.

One way people are conserving energy today is by harvesting energy from wind farms.

Solar panels enable houses to capture energy from the sun.

About 70 percent of all homes in California use energy-saving lightbulbs.

Some scientists are working on a system that uses solar energy to power a house. Their system also uses solar energy to heat water. This hot water is stored as fuel for energy at night. Houses with this system will not have to use electricity from power plants!

In the future, as countries develop and populations grow, we will need more energy. Scientists are trying to learn how to make better use of the energy in our solar system. They want to make sure we will always have all the energy we need! ★

Percentage of electricity provided by nuclear power in the United States: About 20

Percentage of electricity provided by coal in the United States: 44.5 percent

Amount of water Hoover Dam is able to release each second: About 28,400 gal. (107, 500 L)

Speed of sound through air: 1,087 feet (331 m) per second

Speed of light: 186,282,397 miles (299,792,458 km) per second

Percentage of U.S. energy use from renewable solar power in 2008: 0.1 percent

Percentage of U.S. energy use from nonrenewable petroleum in 2008: 37 percent

Did you find the truth?

F The amount of energy in the world changes all the time.

T Sound energy travels faster through water than through air.

Resources

Books

Basher, Simon, and Dan Green. *Chemistry: Getting a Big Reaction!* New York: Kingfisher, 2010.

Boothroyd, Jennifer. *All Charged Up: A Look at Electricity*. Minneapolis: Lerner Publications, 2011.

Bradley, David, and Ian Crofton. *Young Oxford Library of Science: Atoms and Elements*. New York: Oxford University Press, 2002.

Gardner, Robert. *Easy Genius Science Projects With Electricity and Magnetism: Great Experiments and Ideas*. Berkeley Heights, NJ: Enslow Publishers, 2009.

Knapp, Brian. *Simple Electricity*. Vol. 12 of *Science Matters!* New York: Grolier Educational, 2003.

Venezia, Mike. *Albert Einstein: Universal Genius*. New York: Children's Press, 2009.

Organizations and Web Sites

Energy Education Programs

www.energyeducation.tx.gov

Learn about energy, its forms, history, and more from the Texas State Energy Conservation Office.

Physics4Kids.com — Motion Basics

www.physics4kids.com/files/motion_energy.html

Learn about kinetic and potential energy.

U.S. Energy Information Administration — Energy Kids

www.cia.doe.gov/kids/index.cfm

Learn about energy, its sources, and its history.

Places to Visit

American Museum of Science and Energy

300 South Tulane Avenue
Oak Ridge, TN 37830
(865) 576-3200
www.amse.org
See exhibits and participate in programs on energy.

The Bakken Museum

3537 Zenith Avenue South
Minneapolis, MN 55416-4623
(612) 926-3878
www.thebakken.org
Visit exhibits and take workshops on electricity, inventing, and more.

Important Words

electrons (i-LEK-trahnz)—tiny, negatively charged particles that move around the nucleus of an atom

fission (FISH-uhn)—the act of splitting the nucleus of an atom to generate energy

fusion (FYOO-zhuhn)—joining together of the nuclei of two or more atoms to generate energy

hydroelectric power (hy-droh-ih-LEK-trik POW-ur)—electricity generated by using the energy of flowing or falling water

kinetic energy (ki-NET-ik EN-uhr-jee)—energy in motion or use

molecule (MAH-luh-kyool)—the smallest unit a compound can be divided into with all of its chemical properties

neutrons (NOO-trahnz)—one part of the nucleus of an atom; neutrons have no electrical charge

nonrenewable (non-ree-NEW-uh-bul)—unable to be replaced or recreated

nucleus (NOO-klee-uhs)—the central part of an atom that is made up of neutrons and protons

potential energy (po-TEN-chuhl EN-uhr-jee)—energy stored for later use

protons (PROH-tahnz)—positively charged particles inside a nucleus of an atom

renewable (ree-NEW-uh-bul)—able to be replaced or recreated

Index

Page numbers in **bold** indicate illustrations

atoms, 8, **9**, 10, 17, 19, 20, 21, 30, 39, 40

batteries, 17, **18**, **32**
bowling, **24**

chemical energy, 16–17, 23, 37, 38, 40
chemical reactions, 21
coal, 9, **10**, 26, 27, 33
conservation of energy, 40–41
consumption, 41

Edison, Thomas, **33**
Einstein, Albert, **39**
elastic energy, 15
electric eels, **34**
electricity, 7, 9, 10, 18, 21, 27, 32, 33, 34, **35**, 38, 40, 42
electrons, 8, **9**, 17, 32

fission, **21**
food, **16**, 29, **38**
fuel, 7, **10**, **17**, 23, 33, **36**, 42
fusion, 19, 20

geothermal energy, **26**, **31**
gravitational energy, **12**, 13, **14**, 15

heat energy. *See* thermal energy.
Hoover Dam, **35**
hydroelectric power, 35

joules, 15

kinetic energy, **11**, **22**, 23, **24**, 38, 40

lightbulbs, 32, 42
lightning, 32

molecules, **8**, 9, 16, 25, 30
muscles, 34, 38

negative electric charges, 9
neutrons, 8, 19
nonrenewable energy sources, 26, 27
nuclear energy, 19, **21**, 33, 39
nuclei, 8, **9**, 19, 21

oil, 26

playing, **6**, **14**, **15**, **24**, **40**
positive electric charges, 9
potential energy, 10, **11**, **12**, 13, 15, 19, 39
power plants, **21**, **27**, 33, 35, 42
protons, 8, 9, 19

radiant energy, **29**, 37
renewable energy sources, **26**, **27**
Rutherford, Ernest, **19**

sledding, **14**
solar energy, 26, **27**, **29**, 33, **42**
sound energy, **25**, 28
stars, **20**
sunlight, 7
systems, 40, 41–42

thermal energy, **21**, **26**, **30–31**, 33, 37, 38, 42
timeline, **32–33**
turbines, 33

Volta, Alessandro, 18, **32**

water, **8**, 28, 31, 32, 33, 42
water energy, 26, **35**, 37
wind, 24
wind energy, 7, 26, 32, **41**
wood, **17**, 37
work, 7

About the Author

Matt Mullins holds a master's degree in the history of science from the University of Wisconsin–Madison. Formerly a newspaper reporter, he has been a science writer and research consultant for nine years. Matt has written more than two dozen children's books, and has written and directed a few short films. He lives in Madison with his son.